Alfred A. Knopf 🐕 New York

UNBOUND

The Life + Art of Judith Scott

Joyce Scott
with Brie Spangler and Melissa Sweet

Art by Melissa Sweet

THIS IS A BORZOI BOOK PUBLISHED BY ALFRED A. KNOPF

Text copyright © 2021 by Joyce Scott, Brie Spangler, and Melissa Sweet
Jacket art and interior illustrations copyright © 2021 by Melissa Sweet

Judith Scott, 2004 copyright © by Anne Collier. Image courtesy of the artist and Anton Kern Gallery, New York.
Joyce and Judith Scott, age 8, image courtesy of Joyce Scott.
Twins by Judith Scott, image courtesy of John Cooke.
Select art pieces copyright © by Creative Growth Art Center

Visit us on the Web! rhcbooks.com

Educators and librarians, for a variety of teaching tools, visit us at RHTeachersLibrarians.com

Library of Congress Cataloging-in-Publication Data
Names: Scott, Joyce (Joyce Wallace), author. | Spangler, Brie, author. | Sweet, Melissa, illustrator.
Title: Unbound : the life and art of Judith Scott / by Joyce Scott, with Brie Spangler and Melissa Sweet.
Description: First edition. | New York : Alfred A. Knopf, [2021] | "This is a Borzoi book"—Colophon. | Includes bibliographical references. |
Audience: Ages 4–8 | Audience: Grades 2–3 | Summary: "An introduction to the life and art of Judith Scott, a renowned artist."
—provided by publisher
Identifiers: LCCN 2020048702 (print) | LCCN 2020048703 (ebook) | ISBN 978-0-525-64811-6 (hardcover) |
ISBN 978-0-525-64812-3 (library binding) | ISBN 978-0-525-64813-0 (ebook)
Subjects: LCSH: Scott, Judith, 1943–2005—Juvenile literature. | Down syndrome patients as artists—United States—
Biography—Juvenile literature. | Deaf artists—United States—Biography—Juvenile literature. |
Sisters—United States—Biography—Juvenile literature. | Twins—United States—Biography—Juvenile literature.
Classification: LCC NB237.S3868 S36 2021 (print) | LCC NB237.S3868
(ebook) | DDC 730.92 [B]—dc23

The text of this book is set in 16-point Argone LC.
The illustrations were created using watercolor, colored pencil, mixed media,
found objects, wood, yarn, thread, and twine.
Book design by Nicole de las Heras

MANUFACTURED IN CHINA
June 2021
10 9 8 7 6 5

First Edition

For Judy, my teacher and my twin
—J.S.

To my family, thank you always
—B.S.

To Paul W. Hankins, artist and teacher, Room 407
—M.S.

ENTWINED

Before we know the touch of air on our skin, my sister and I know each other.

Judy and I are twins, and we are each other's world. We share everything— our mom, our dad, our three older brothers, and our home. Together, under the sun, the moon, and the stars, it's all we know, and we are happy.

We sleep like spoons nestled in a drawer.

We play inside with twin dolls and a pair of tiny teacups. Outside we have matching pails for making mudpies and mulberry soup.

I don't know if everything comes in twos, but it seems that way to me!

Most days, neighborhood kids come and go. We circle around each other's backyards until our parents call us in for supper.

No matter where we are, Judy wants to do what I'm doing. Mom says we're two peas in a pod.

On warm nights, we play on an old outdoor couch, with our upside-down selves lying close together like tiny explorers of the universe.

Between the blue sea below and a million stars above to guide us,
Judy's eyes are wide, and she squeezes my arm with both her hands.

Soon I begin kindergarten.

Mom tries to enroll Judy in school, but she has special needs that keep her home. Judy has what will come to be known as Down syndrome; she was born with an extra chromosome buried deep inside. The doctors said she would have learning disabilities and that her heart was not as strong as it should be.

BUS STOP

Judy has never spoken a word. We wonder if she will
ever talk. The doctors say that she is slow and will not
get better, but they don't know Judy like I do. She is perfect
just the way she is. She knows things that no one else
knows and sees the world in ways that I never will.

THE COLORS OF GONE

One day, I wake up and reach for my sister, but she is gone. I look for her everywhere. Daddy is gone, too.

  I find Mommy in the kitchen, sitting alone. She tells me Judy's gone away. Daddy took her to a special school, where she'll live now. The teachers there will help her learn to talk.

That night, Daddy returns.

I hide in the hall and listen as he tells Mommy how hard it was to leave Judy. I know how sad Judy must have been because now I feel sad, too.

And just like that, my whole world disappears and is replaced with the colors of gone.

Our room stays the same—Judy's magazines, dolls, plastic zoo animals, and wooden blocks are scattered everywhere. Mommy puts Judy's toys in a box, but I won't let her take them away.

Every night, I pile the toys beside me on the bed and feel each one in the dark, thinking about Judy's hands holding them.

Finally, my parents take me to visit my sister. I wear my
yellow dress just like Judy's and hope she'll wear hers, too,
so everyone will know we're twins. I pack her a magazine
with pictures of bunnies that I know she will love.

OFFICE

But when we arrive, I don't understand . . .
this place can't be a school.

There's no playground, no desks or books, no chalkboards, crayons, or colored paper.

Judy and I hug each other tight; then she sits right on the floor, pulling me down with her. She wants to look at the magazine. I find the bunny page for her, and she likes it a lot. I knew she would.

I clutch Judy close and say "Hi" in a loud voice. I am desperate for her to learn to speak. Judy replies, "Ho, ho, bah," and pats my face.

From that day on, in my mind, even though we are apart, Judy doesn't stay inside that horrible gray place. She stays outside with me, breathing in the colors of our world.

UNBOUND

The years turn, and each time I visit my sister, I can't bear to say goodbye. I bring friends to meet Judy. Later, my husband meets her, and then my children.

But as time goes on, I'm now living so far away that distance keeps us apart. Yet I still dream of her by my side.

I decide it is time. I call Judy's institution in Ohio to tell them I want her to come live with me in California. I need to know everything about her so I can be ready for our life together.

I press the phone hard to my ear. A woman tells me how difficult it is to care for my twin, especially because she's deaf. What does she mean *deaf*?

She tells me that Judy may have been deaf most of her life. How could she be deaf and we didn't know? Is this why she has never talked?

Then I remember moments from our childhood—
Judy running down the street, with all of us shouting
at her while she keeps going.

JUDY!

JUDY!

JUDY!

JOYCE AND JUDY!

JUDY

She needed my touch to stop when
my parents called us inside.

Judy's records arrive before she does. They read: not appropriate for any educational program, behaviorial problems, unmanageable.

How dare they label my sister and deny her the right to learn? They don't know Judy like I do.

JUDY 1948

Records

AUG 1 0 ENT'D

Report for week end
Examined and

JUDITH SCOTT

S

Institute of
Columbus
Ohio

NOTICE OF MISCONDUCT

WE
RE

MON

TUE

WED

THUR

FRI.

during

Parent

TO BE CONFIRMED

OCT 2 6 P.M.

MONDAY
19

TUESDAY
20
JUDY ARRIVES!

WEDNESDAY
21

THURSDAY
22

Finally, the day comes. The institution promises me that someone will accompany Judy on her first-ever flight. But waiting at the airport with my family, I see the last person off the plane is a lone figure, small and stooped, in the distance. I rush toward her. My sister drops her purse and magazines and melts into my arms. My daughter slips in between us, and she too holds Judy, while my husband wraps his arms around the bundle that is us.

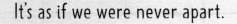

It's as if we were never apart.

A NEW LANGUAGE

Judy is happy; we are all happy. But I know that she needs a place to learn, to be with people, especially while I am away from home each day, working as a nurse.

I hear about a local art studio, Creative Growth Art Center, that offers programs for adults with disabilities. The artists are encouraged to express themselves using whatever materials they choose.

OAKLAND

I have no idea if Judy will like being there. I am not aware of her making
anything ever, not even a drawing.

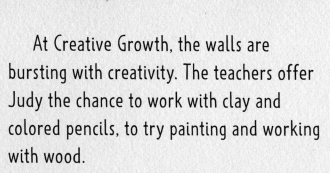

At Creative Growth, the walls are bursting with creativity. The teachers offer Judy the chance to work with clay and colored pencils, to try painting and working with wood.

Many months go by, but nothing interests her. Judy only wants to look at her magazines.

I worry that she may not be allowed to stay if she isn't making art.

Then one day, Judy watches a teacher spread out all sorts of natural materials. The teacher encourages Judy to join in.

Judy picks delicate willow twigs and winds them together with yarn and twine, weaving in odd bits of wood. She secures the bundle with nails and colorful pins, then paints it.

And just like that, a form emerges.
Her teachers are encouraged! We're all encouraged. Judy has made something as unique as she is.

The next day, she makes another form and then another. From that moment on, every morning, Judy bursts into Creative Growth and goes directly to her place in the studio, sets her magazines on a chair, and begins working.

Judy chooses colored yarns and fibers, chunks of wood, and a shopping cart for her art. Sometimes, as she forages the studio for materials, Judy "borrows" a tool, someone's keys, or eyeglasses, and weaves these objects deep into her work.

When a piece is complete, my sister gives a thumbs-up, pats it, pushes it away, and begins another.

For years, Judy wraps and weaves, creating fantastic, cocoon-like shapes filled with color.

She wraps her head in beautiful hats, scarves, and ribbons, becoming her own work of art.

Then one day, she makes a new piece unlike any other: small and black, all the colors gone.
 Judy hands me her stack of beloved magazines.

The next day, Judy dies in my arms. Though my sister died of heart failure, she lived much longer than anyone expected, or could have hoped for.

When she leaves this world, my sister is celebrated as a great artist.
Her fame still grows.

My twin and I shared a love as deep and wide as the starry night.
We are two hearts forever entwined.

TYING LOOSE ENDS

After being confined to an institution for thirty-five years, Judy began a new life in California, where she attended the Creative Growth Art Center in Oakland for the final eighteen years of her life. Here she worked five days a week, creating more than 160 sculptures. As interest, even amazement, in Judy's sculptures swelled, Creative Growth arranged several shows of her work. Judy soon became an internationally recognized fiber artist. Her work has been shown in museums around the world, including in New York, London, Paris, Dublin, Tokyo, and Lausanne, Switzerland. Other artists at Creative Growth have achieved similar recognition and fame.

Creative Growth is the first art studio of its kind for people with disabilities to explore, develop, and communicate their own creativity. The center is described as a "model for a creative community guided by the principle that art is fundamental to human expression and that all people are entitled to its tools of communication." They have inspired similar art centers all over the world. Most important, the artists there are recognized not for their limitations, but for their vast potential. Judy's life and legacy embody that truth.

DOWN SYNDROME

Down syndrome is a genetic disorder caused by being born with an extra chromosome. Chromosomes contain the genes that carry all the information necessary for our bodies to develop and maintain themselves.

Often children with Down syndrome take a longer time learning to speak. Some will have heart problems, hearing issues, and physical delays, but with education and support, most people with Down syndrome today will live happy and productive lives.

The life expectancy for people born with Down syndrome is also much longer today than when Judith Scott was born. Despite the grim statistics, Judy outlived her life expectancy by fifty years.

Photograph of Judith Scott by Anne Collier, 2004

TIMELINE

1943: Joyce and Judith Scott are born on May 1 in Cincinnati, Ohio.

1948: Joyce begins kindergarten.

1950: Judith's parents place her in the Columbus State Institution on the advice of her doctor.

1969: Joyce moves to California, where she works as a teacher and later a nurse.

1973: The Rehabilitation Act of 1973 is passed, giving people with disabilities equal access to programs, services, activities, and facilities that receive federal financial assistance.

1974: Creative Growth Art Center is founded by Florence Ludins-Katz and Elias Katz in Oakland, California. It is the oldest and largest nonprofit art studio for artists with developmental, intellectual, and physical disabilities.

Joyce and Judith Scott, age 8

1977: The Lanterman Act is passed, giving people with developmental disabilities the right to services and supports that enable them to live a more independent and normal life.

1985: Joyce begins the lengthy process of becoming Judith's legal guardian.

1985: Judith moves to California to be with Joyce and her family.

1987: Judith begins attending Creative Growth Art Center in Oakland.

1989: Sylvia Seventy, fiber artist and instructor at Creative Growth Art Center, facilitates Judith's first piece of art using fiber materials and found objects.

1990: The Americans with Disabilities Act is signed into law, ensuring that people with disabilities have the same rights and opportunities as everyone else.

1999: The first show of Judith's work takes place, coinciding with the publication of *Metamorphosis: The Fiber Art of Judith Scott,* written by John M. MacGregor.

2003: A documentary film crew x-rays Judith's work to examine its construction and finds that objects are hidden inside.

2005: Judith dies on March 15 of heart failure.

Photograph on right: *Twins* by Judith Scott

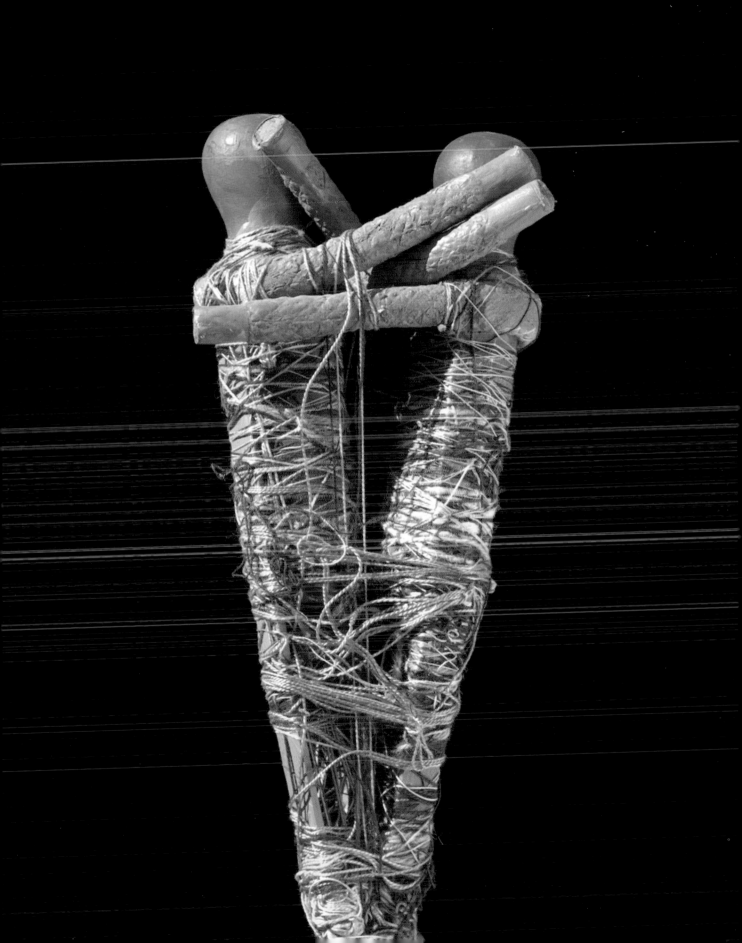

AUTHOR NOTE

Wherever we live, we find many people who are a bit "different" in one way or another. These individuals, because of their differences, are often thought of as being less than those of us who consider ourselves "normal." They are often kept at a distance, not included in the everydayness of our lives—sharing laughter and meals, bus rides and work, cozy couch time and a welcome night's sleep. Because they are not valued, their unseen strengths and gifts often go unrecognized, unexplored, and undiscovered.

Creative Growth is a place that challenges these false perceptions. It is a place that welcomes and includes people who have been dismissed because of some obvious difference and perceived limitations. At Creative Growth, people are given a chance to explore their own creativity and possibilities, and to find their voice.

In an environment like this, it's easy to see that there are no people without the gift of creativity and without a voice for singing, once given an opportunity to sing and be heard. Creative Growth artists sing through their paintings, weavings, and pottery, and we are all the richer for these newfound, undiscovered voices.

One of the greatest riches in my life has been to be Judy's twin, her heart so deep, her kindness without end. One of her blessings was being an artist at Creative Growth, where she gave the world new expressions of beauty and, in the process, found a voice and a song all her own.

ILLUSTRATOR NOTE

What drew me to Judith Scott's story was learning that for most of her life she had no opportunity to be creative, but when given the chance, Judith created not only something extraordinary, but showed a resilient spirit.

The paintings and collages for this book were created with watercolor, colored pencils, and mixed media. In order to convey Judith's process and art, I interpreted her work with found objects, wood, yarn, thread, and twine. Some of the pages include art by students from the Creative Growth Art Center within the collages. I'm grateful to be able to include their work.

On a research trip to California, I met with fiber artist Sylvia Seventy, the teacher who inspired Judith to make her first wrapped pieces. Many thanks to Sylvia for graciously sharing photos and stories about Judith's process. Thanks, too, to instructor Tara Tucker for her time and insights.

Making this book was a collaboration, and I'm grateful to my colleagues—editor Erin Clarke, art director Nicole de las Heras, and authors Joyce Scott and Brie Spangler—for their generosity. Thank you.

SOURCES

Barrera, Iola, and Iñaki Peñafiel, directors. *What's Under Your Hat? (¿Qué tienes debajo del sombrero?)*. Cinema Guild, 2007.

Bayha, Betsy, director. *Outsider: The Life and Art of Judith Scott*. Fanlight Productions, 2014.

The Creative Growth Book: From the Outside to the Inside—Artists with Disabilities Today. Milan: 5 Continents, 2019.

"Creative Growth—Judith Scott." *Creative Growth*, 2020. creativegrowth.org

MacGregor, John M. *Metamorphosis: The Fiber Art of Judith Scott*. Oakland, CA: Creative Growth Art Center, 1999.

Morris, Catherine, and Matthew Higgs, editors. *Judith Scott: Bound and Unbound*. New York: Prestel, 2014.

Scott, Joyce Wallace. *Entwined: Sisters and Secrets in the Silent World of Artist Judith Scott*. Boston: Beacon Press, 2016.

ORGANIZATIONS

Down Syndrome International, Global Down Syndrome Foundation,
National Down Syndrome Congress, National Down Syndrome Society.